WING CHU
JEET KUN
A COMPARISON Vol. 1
by William Cheung
and Ted Wong

Editor: Mike Lee
Graphic Design: Sergio Onaga
Photography: Doug Churchill

©1990 Ohara Publications, Inc.
All rights reserved
Printed in the United States of America
Library of Congress Catalog Card Number: 90-063463
ISBN 0-89750-124-1

Seventh printing 2000

WARNING

This book is presented only as a means of preserving a unique aspect of the heritage of the martial arts. Neither Ohara Publications nor the author makes any representation, warranty or guarantee that the techniques described or illustrated in this book will be safe or effective in any self-defense situation or otherwise. You may be injured if you apply or train in the techniques of self-defense illustrated in this book, and neither Ohara Publications nor the author is responsible for any such injury that may result. It is essential that you consult a physician regarding whether or not to attempt any technique described in this book. Specific self-defense responses illustrated in this book may not be justified in any particular situation in view of all of the circumstances or under the applicable federal, state or local law. Neither Ohara Publications nor the author makes any representation or warranty regarding the legality or appropriateness of any technique mentioned in this book.

OHARA  PUBLICATIONS, INCORPORATED
SANTA CLARITA. CALIFORNIA

DEDICATION

Wing Chun Kung Fu/Jeet Kune Do: A Comparison is dedicated to the memory of its editor Mike Lee. A gentleman, a scholar, and a dear friend, Mike will be sorely missed by all those who knew him.

ACKNOWLEDGEMENTS

For their help in preparing this book, William Cheung acknowledges his students Ken Teichmann and Raymond Mar. Ted Wong acknowledges the help of his students Mark Wong, Tommy Gong, and his son, Brice Wong.

ABOUT THE AUTHOR: WILLIAM CHEUNG

William Cheung was born in 1940 in Hong Kong. He is regarded as one of today's most proficient martial artists. By dint of a strange set of circumstances, he is the inheritor of a devastatingly effective fighting style…*wing chun kung ku*.

Wing chun is a unique martial arts system developed by a woman in China almost 300 years ago. Because it was developed by a woman, it does not emphasize the use of brute force and strength, but rather concentrates on developing an effective training system to improve the practitioner's balance, reflexes and co-ordination.

Cheung has had over 40 years' experience in wing chun and stands eighth in the direct line of grandmasters from its originator, Ng Mui. In 1959, Cheung left Hong Kong to pursue an academic career in Australia, and graduated from the Australian National University in Canberra as Bachelor of Arts and Economics.

In 1973 Cheung decided to teach martial arts professionally in Australia, and set up his headquarters in Melbourne's Chinatown. During 1974, he founded the Australian Wing Chun Academy in Melbourne and he saw to the founding of the Australian Kung Fu Federation.

In the period from 1978 to 1980, Cheung was appointed chief instructor in

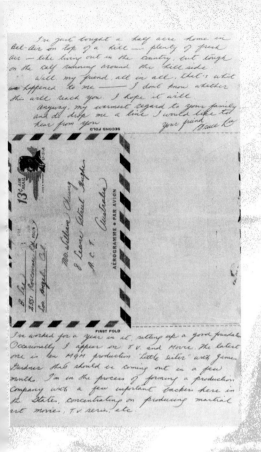

unarmed combat to the U.S. Marines of the Seventh Fleet, based in Yokosuka, Japan.

Cheung was awarded the *Black Belt* Hall of Fame award, "Kung Fu Artist of the Year," in 1983 and in the following year he set the world speed punching record of 8.3 punches per second at Harvard University.

He is the author of ten books on the martial art of wing chun kung fu and has appeared in the cover stories of numerous international magazines. In 1987, he starred in his first instructional videotape, *The Wing Chun Way,* a product of the Hawk Company in Hollywood.

In November, 1988, he opened his new international headquarters situated in the heart of the southeastern region of Melbourne, Victoria. This unique 24,000-square-foot center is one of the most technically advanced martial arts training centers in the world.

He is the president of the Australian National Kung Fu Federation, and chairman of the World Wing Chun Kung Fu Assocation, and has lectured on the art of wing chun in Los Angeles, Las Vegas, Sacramento, Boston, Chicago, New York, London, Paris, Auckland as well as across Australia.

BRUCE LEE'S JEET KUNE DO
截拳道

以無限爲有限

以無法爲有法

This is to certify that

Ted Wong

Is personally taught by Bruce Lee, and having fulfilled the necessary requirements is hereby promoted to 2nd *rank in Jeet Kune Do.*

Date Dec. 8 1967

ABOUT THE AUTHOR: TED WONG

Over the past 15 years, the term *jeet kune do* has become a common household word in martial arts, made famous by its late founder, Bruce Lee. Although not until recently has Ted Wong made public his interpretation of jeet kune do, he has been privately training and teaching a few students ever since the death of his teacher. Today, he is one of the very few JKD practitioners who can trace his roots directly to the founder.

Wong actually began JKD in 1967 at Bruce Lee's third *kwoon* (training hall) in Los Angeles' Chinatown. Later on, Lee took him as a private student and workout partner, becoming one of only four people to have been personally trained by Bruce Lee and groomed for instructorship; the others being Taky Kimura, the late James Lee, and Dan Inosanto. In addition, among the many students of Bruce Lee, Ted Wong was one of only two people to have received certificates in jeet kune do, the other being Dan Inosanto. Most of Lee's students received the Jun Fan Gung Fu Institute certificate, which states that the students achieved rank according to the standards of the Jun Fan Gung Fu Institute (the name of Bruce Lee's schools in Seattle, Oakland, and Los Angeles.) But the jeet kune do certificate states that one must have been personally taught by Bruce Lee in order to have received rank in JKD. Wong trained with Bruce Lee toward the

end of Lee's later stages of JKD development, basically becoming Lee's last major private student.

Ted Wong was also one of the primary people involved with demonstrating techniques in the photos used in both the *Bruce Lee's Fighting Method* series of books co-authored by Bruce Lee and M. Uyehara, and the book *Wing Chun Kung Fu*, authored by the late James Lee, edited by Bruce Lee.

After Lee's death, Wong chose not to teach JKD openly to the public. He maintained a low profile, keeping almost entirely out of the public eye. He continued to train in the backyard as he had previously done with Lee with a few friends like Herb Jackson, further developing his JKD skills in private. He has taken very few students over the years, and only then on a private, personal one-to-one basis with the student. In addition, Wong has continued numerous semi-private seminars in Los Angeles and San Francisco the last few years.

Ted Wong established a semi-private, non-profit jeet kune do school in San Francisco in 1990. The school's objective, being part of the program taught at the Chung Ngai Dance Troupe in Chinatown, is to preserve and proliferate JKD in its purest sense. Originally, the Chung Ngai Dance Troupe was established for underprivileged teenagers in the 1960s. Wong also felt that since JKD has not really been exposed to the Chinese community, this endeavor would give something back to Bruce Lee's birthplace, heritage, and culture during the founder's 50th birthday anniversary.

ORIGINS OF WING CHUN KUNG FU

The origin of wing chun kung fu can be found in the turbulent, repressive Ching dynasty of over 250 years ago. It was a time when 90 percent of the Chinese race, the Hons, were ruled by the ten percent minority, the Manchus. The Manchus placed a great amount of unjust law on the Hons. For instance, all the female Hon infants were made to bind their feet so that when they grew up they would be dependent upon their parents or husband. The work opportunity of the Hons was also restricted. They were unable to hold office in government higher than a certain level. Heavy tax burdens were placed on the country so that the Manchus could have economic control of the Hon people. Kung fu training was also banned for the Hons, however the Manchu government was adopting the Hon culture. They respected the Shil Lim Temple as a Buddhist sanctuary.

When all weapons were outlawed by the Manchus, the Hons began training a revolutionary army in the secret art of kung fu. The Shil Lim Temple became the secret sanctuary for the preparatory training of the classic style which took 15 to 20 years for each person to master.

To develop a new form, one which would have shorter training time, five of China's grandmasters met to discuss the merits of each of the various forms of kung fu. By choosing the most efficient techniques from each style, they developed training programs that would develop an efficient martial artist in five to seven years, one third of the original time. However before this new form could be put into practice, the Shil Lim Temple was raided and burned by the Manchus.

Ng Mui, a nun, was the only survivor of the original five grandmasters. She passed her knowledge on to a young orphan girl whom she named Wing Chun. The name represented "hope for the future." In turn, Wing Chun passed her knowledge on to her husband. Through the years, the style became known as wing chun. Its techniques and teachings were passed on to a few, always carefully selected, students.

In 1950, Yip Man started to teach wing chun in Hong Kong. One of his first students was William Cheung, now the head of the World Traditional Wing Chun Kung Fu Association.

ORIGINS OF JEET KUNE DO

Although this book deals solely with wing chun and jeet kune do, it is advisable to research the whole spectrum of Bruce Lee's martial arts in the context of his life in general, from his beginnings in wing chun to his modifications with Jun Fan kung fu (or, as he called it, "gung fu"), to his own discovery of jeet kune do. In order to fully understand jeet kune do, you must understand Bruce Lee.

Lee's martial arts began in Hong Kong, where he learned wing chun as a tireless youngster, practicing the direct and economical close-range techniques of that style every chance he got. He trained diligently with his sifu, Yip Man, and seniors William Cheung and Wong Shun Leung, but his training was cut short when, at the age of 18, his parents sent him to America to claim his United States citizenship.

After a brief stay in San Francisco, his birthplace, Bruce moved to Seattle, Washington, to live with a family friend. It was at this time he began to modify his classical wing chun method. Bruce began to adjust the stances, angles, and positions of his wing chun techniques, also adding longer-range kicking techniques from some of the northern kung fu styles. Among notable people who learned from Bruce in this time period is Taky Kimura.

After his marriage to Linda Emery, Bruce moved to Oakland, California, to live with James Lee and his family. James was a very good friend, and they had daily contact with each other during his stay in Oakland. Bruce continued to make minor changes to his modified wing chun style, which he called Jun Fan gung fu out of respect for traditional wing chun and his sifu, Yip Man, in Hong Kong.

The well-known fight with Wong Jak Man is considered the turning point which led Bruce to the development of jeet kune do. Until Wong Jak Man, Bruce had been content with improvising and expanding on his original wing chun, but after the altercation, Bruce judged that the modified system had limited his performance. He concluded that a strict adherence to wing chun was too confining for him because it had very few long-range kicks. He also found that he had become quite tired after the fight. He therefore began to add new dimensions to his art. He searched for the best within himself. He also studied other fighting arts, and from these researches, he absorbed what was useful and rejected what was useless. This became the basis of jeet kune do at a higher level. It could be concluded that the seeds of jeet kune do were implanted by this event.

Bruce then moved to Los Angeles to be closer to the entertainment industry. At first he trained only a few students behind a pharmacy in Chinatown. Among them was Dan Inosanto. This was in 1967. It was the third of the Jun Fan Gung Fu Institutes, the first two being in Seattle and Oakland, respectively. By the time Lee came to Los Angeles, he had decided to scrap his modified wing chun (Jun Fan gung fu) and search out the roots of combat, to find the universal principles and concepts fundamental to all styles and systems.

Bruce emphasized wing chun less and less because of its perceived limitations. Lee found it difficult, for example, to practice *chi sao* (sticking hands) with Kareem Abdul Jabbar, the seven foot plus basketball star, who was, at the time, the center for the University of California at Los Angeles. The length of his arms made him difficult to hit. Size was still too much of a factor. He also found that although the sensitivity in the arms developed by wing chun training allowed him good defenses in close range, it did not completely eliminate the threat of being hit. He found, however, that staying outside the opponent's effective range did eliminate that threat, and he could still hit the opponent because of his superior gap-bridging skills.

The training in Los Angeles was very contact-oriented, utilizing striking pads for practice, and body armor for full-contact sparring. All techniques were geared toward realistic combat on the street. Conditioning was also heavily emphasized to solve the problem of fatigue encountered in his fight with Wong Jak Man.

At this point, it should be emphasized that Ted Wong's interpretation of jeet kune do is by no means completely representative of Bruce's Lee's entire martial arts progression. Wong learned from Lee during the later years of his development when his martial art was changing even more rapidly than before. The greatest contrast between students of Bruce Lee is seen between Taky Kimura, one of Lee's earliest students, and Wong, one of his last. You would not think that both were taught by the same teacher, yet both claim to keep Lee's teaching as pure as possible. The movements each was taught were merely what Lee felt was important at the time they each studied with him, so that not Taky Kimura's, not Dan Inosanto's, and not Ted Wong's interpretations of jeet kune do are fully representative of Lee's martial arts spectrum.

Dan Inosanto, however, is one of the people most responsible for keeping the jeet kune do flame alive. He has done a great deal to expose the art of jeet kune do to the entire world by holding seminars and writing articles and books since the passing of their teacher. Were it not for Dan, jeet kune do might possibly have died with Bruce Lee. Dan has also gone into his own roots, searching out the many Filipino martial arts, and many of the Southeast Asian arts, and offering his students jeet kune do concepts through the interpretation of other vehicles such as *kali*, *muay Thai*, and *pentjak silat*. His art is considered an added dimension in the jeet kune do time-line. Dan has followed his own light, and found the best within himself.

Although Bruce disliked the word "style," for describing jeet kune do, there was a distinctive character to his way of fighting and training which was unlike any other martial art. In order to preserve this art, jeet kune do has to become somewhat of a style in the sense of being standardized and systematized, because unless some kind of structure is imposed on it, it will not survive in its original forms. Bruce did not have any plans on how to preserve jeet kune do, so it is the responsibility of his elder students to offer the present and future generations the experience of the original training, formulas, principles, and progression of jeet kune do. A teacher should provide the foundation for the student, then offer his own interpretations, and assist the student to find his own best way.

Wing chun does indeed form the foundation of jeet kune do in concept, but not in character. There are many wing chun principles in jeet kune do which were taken completely unaltered or were modified: economy of motion, directness, simultaneous attack and defense, non-opposition of force, the centerline, and the four corners. But Bruce also added many new dimensions to his system. His fighting method eventually diverged so far from wing chun, he renamed it jeet kune do.

Table of Contents

Chapter 1

STANCES AND FOOTWORK

While wing chun uses three basic stances, jeet kune do uses only one. Wing chun uses the neutral stance, the neutral side stance, and the forward stance. There is one intermediary stance which is more of a step used when changing stances. This is sometimes called the T-stance where the feet are brought together, one placed behind the other at a 90-degree angle.

A retreating step is also used in wing chun. Here, the rear leg is used as a pivot, and the front foot is swung a full step back into the rear position on a line behind the pivot foot, and the body is turned completely sideways. This retreating move is usually accompanied by a defensive arm technique such as *bon sao* or *fut sao*.

Both wing chun and jeet kune do use sidesteps to change attacking angles and as an evasion technique, although the steps used are different. Jeet kune do also uses shuffling steps to chase or retreat, as well as a sudden backward step called a pendulum step for quick evasion of a long-range technique such as a kick.

In jeet kune do, 80 percent of all striking is done with the lead hand or foot. Therefore, you should put your strong side forward. This concept makes jeet kune do structurally fast. If your right hand is stronger, for example, and has more endurance, speed, and coordination, you should use it the most. But if it is the rear position, then you are structurally slow, because although you want to strike with it most of the time, it will have a longer distance to travel, and you will always telegraph your motion.

You will also expose your centerline and groin with a rear weapon attack. Every time you throw a rear weapon, the whole front of your body is exposed, leaving very vulnerable targets open to your opponent. Also because your left hand is weaker, you need it in the rear position, so that you can give it a chance to gain momentum for added power.

In boxing, you put the right hand in the rear to create a more powerful weapon in the right cross. Granted, the boxing right cross is more powerful than the lead right or left cross, but the speed obtained by using the stronger hand in the lead position outweighs the benefit of the right cross.

In this case then, the strongest weapon is thrown at the closest target with maximum speed and economy of motion, giving the opponent little chance of reacting to your attack. The same reasoning applies to kicking.

Wing Chun Stances

There are three basic stances in wing chun, the neutral stance, the neutral side stance, and the front stance.

In the wing chun neutral stance, the feet are even with each other and placed one step apart, with toes pointed straight ahead, and weight distributed evenly on both feet. The left neutral stance is distinguished by having the left hand in the lead position, while the right neutral stance leads with the right hand.

In the wing chun neutral side stance, the feet are also a normal stepping distance apart, and your weight is distributed evenly on both feet. In the right neutral side stance, the right foot points straight ahead, the right hand leads, and the left leg is turned at the hip so the left foot and knee point 75 degrees to the left. In the left neutral side stance, the left foot points straight ahead and the left hand leads.

In the wing chun front stance, your back foot points outward 75 degrees from the forward direction, and your front foot is turned slightly inward so that your front knee protects the groin. The distance between your feet is a normal step, and your weight is distributed evenly on both feet. In the right front stance, the right foot is in front with the right hand in the lead, and in the left front stance, the left foot is in front with the left hand in the lead.

Left Neutral Stance

Right Neutral Stance

Neutral Side Stance

Right Neutral Side Stance

Front Stance

Right Front Stance

Jeet Kune Do Stance

The most effective jeet kune do stance for both attacking and defending is the on-guard position. As in photos A, B, and C, assume a semi-crouch position, with your weight distributed evenly on both feet, and kept at a comfortable distance apart for good balance. The rear heel is raised and cocked for greater mobility. The lead foot and leg are turned inward so the trunk forms a straight line with the leading leg. This presents a narrow target to the opponent. The rear hand is held high, elbow and forearm close to the body for protection. The rear hand is relied on heavily for defense. The lead hand is held slightly lower with the shoulder and arm loose and relaxed. The lead hand and foot are heavily depended on for striking. In combat, it is important to apply all weapons offensively as well as defensively from the on-guard position, and to return to the on-guard position as quickly as possible.

A

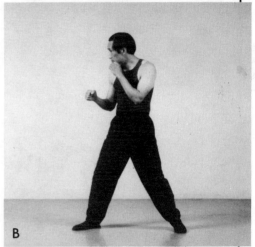

B

C

Wing Chun Sidestepping

The wing chun sidesteps use the technique of bringing both feet together to form a T-stance. From the T-stance, the practitioner has the option of stepping out directly to the left or right to establish a new neutral side stance, or diagonally forward to establish a front stance. In application, this means greater mobility than the modified wing chun system which does not have the T-stance.

Wing Chun Left Sidestep

(1) Starting with a left neutral side stance, (2&3) step across with the right foot, and place it behind the left foot.

Application of the Wing Chun Left Sidestep

(1&2) In this example, the opponent attempts a round kick. The defender sidesteps to the left into the temporary T-stance, and executes the block. Then, (3) he steps diagonally forward into a front stance to land a counter to the face.

Wing Chun Right Sidestep

(1) From a left neutral side stance, (2) bring the left foot in position behind the right foot, and (3) adjust the position of the right foot to form a T-stance.

Application of the Wing Chun Right Sidestep

(1) From the left neutral side stance, the defender (2) sidesteps to the right to avoid the kick, forming a T-stance from which he (3) steps diagonally forward into a front stance and lands his counter.

Jeet Kune Do
Sidestepping

Jeet kune do's on-guard stance establishes "outside" and "inside" as the best way to describe jeet kune do sidestepping because the stance is so strongly sideward to begin with. Stepping to the outside is a simple step outward with the front foot. Then the rear foot is brought in alignment behind it to establish a new on-guard stance. But, stepping inward, the rear foot moves first, taking an inward step, and then the front foot is brought into alignment with the rear foot. The reason is easy to see. Stepping to the inside with the front foot first or stepping to the outside

Jeet Kune Do
Left Sidestep

(1) From the on-guard position, (2) move the left rear foot sharply to the left a distance of about 18 inches. (The same step may also be performed directly to the left and forward.) (3) Slide the right lead foot an equal distance to the left and back to the on-guard position.

ith the rear foot first places
e body in a very disadvanta-
eous position with respect to
e opponent. You are exposed,
hile the effective range of
ur techniques is focused off
an angle. This is also a major
ncern in wing chun as you
ill see in the chapter called
"actics" where correct and
correct foot placement is dis-
ssed. For the sake of de-
ribing these examples of jeet
ne do sidestepping, it will be
sumed that the right side is
e strong side, and that in the
t kune do on-guard stance,
e right side faces the oppo-
nt.

Application of the Jeet Kune Do Left Sidestep

(1) From the on-guard position, (2) sidestep to the left to
evade the attack as the opponent attempts a front punch.

Jeet Kune Do
Right Sidestep

(1) From the on-guard position, (2) move the right lead foot sharply to the right a distance of about 18 inches. (The same step may also be performed diagonally to the right and forward.) (3) Slide the left rear foot an equal distance behind the right and back to the on-guard position.

Application of the Jeet Kune Do Right Sidestep

(1) From the on-guard position, (2) sidestep to the right to evade the attack as the opponent attempts a rear cross.

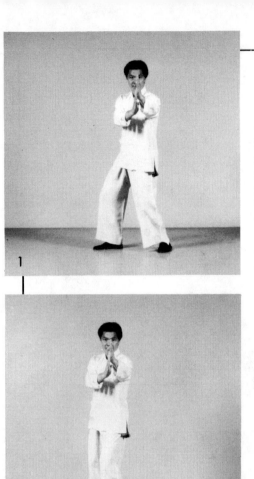

Wing Chun Forward Stepping

Wing chun teaches that in stepping forward, the stepping foot is first brought through the middle, close to the support foot, before stepping diagonally forward into the front stance. The reason for this is to insure "interruptability." If circumstances change in the middle of taking a forward step, an alternate step can be taken in any direction because the feet are close together, and either of the feet can become the pivot foot or support foot for a subsequent step.

Jeet kune do has two methods of advancing, the advance shuffle, and the quick advance. The movements are the same, the forward leg steps ahead first, and the rear leg slides up from behind the appropriate distance to establish the new on-guard position. However, the distance covered in one step is very different. In the advance shuffle, the front foot steps forward a full half step. In the quick advance, the front foot steps forward only about four

Wing Chun Forward Step

(1) From a left neutral side stance, (2) lift the left foot, and bring it through the center before (3) stepping diagonally forward into a front stance.

inches. The forward shuffle is used to advance by increments with some caution, while the quick advance is generally used to strike because there is an opening.

Wing chun exercises prudence by bringing the feet together for all forward steps, whereas jeet kune do exercises prudence by having not only a fully committed forward half step with no intermediate move, but also a shorter, quicker forward shift that gives up little in the way of safety; and in both, the rear foot slides forward maintaining a closeness to the ground which also allows for interruptability.

Jeet kune do forward stepping is comparable to the method of forward stepping of the modified wing chun system in that the rear foot slides up from behind to establish a new stance. In contrast, traditional wing chun teaches never to drag or slide the feet, but to pick them up and plant them each time they are moved.

Application of the Wing Chun Forward Step

(1) The defender executes his block from a left neutral side stance, then (2) steps diagonally forward into a front stance to land his counter.

Jeet Kune Do Advance Shuffle

(1) From the on-guard position, (2) execute the advance shuffle by stepping with the lead foot forward about half a step, then (3) slide the rear foot forward to form a new on-guard position.

Application of the Jeet Kune Do Advance Shuffle

(1) Facing the opponent in the on-guard position, the defender attempts to close the distance. (2) He takes a half step forward with his forward leg, then (3) slides the rear foot forward to establish a new on-guard position.

3

3

Retreat Steps

Wing chun uses a backward step to execute a retreat coupled with a simultaneous blocking maneuver. As the front foot steps to the rear, the leading hand also shifts to the rear position, and the other hand takes the lead to execute the block.

Wing Chun Backward Step

(1) From a front stance, (2) bring your forward foot back alongside the support foot. (3) Step back diagonally, and at the same time bring the rear arm into the lead, and withdraw the lead arm into the rear position.

Jeet kune do uses three kinds of retreats, the retreat shuffle, the quick retreat, both of which are reverse versions of the advance shuffle and quick advance respectively. The third kind of retreat used in jeet kune do is the pendulum step.

Application of the Wing Chun Backward Step

(1) The defender faces the attacker in a left front stance. (2) The attacker punches, and the defender blocks with his lead arm. (3) The attacker steps forward and attempts another punch. The defender steps back with his left foot, and bringing his right arm into the lead, executes another block.

1

2

3

Jeet Kune Do Quick Advance

(1) From the on-guard position, (2) take a fast and sudden small step forward three to four inches with the front foot. (3) Quickly slide the rear foot forward almost to replace the front foot position. (4) Just before the rear foot makes contact with the front, slide on the front foot forward to form a new on-guard position. The purpose of the quick advance is to use a series of these steps to cover ground rapidly and to bridge the gap without deviating from the on-guard position. The quick advance can also be used to intitiate a fast and deep penetrating attack.

4

Application of the Jeet Kune Do
Quick Advance

(1) From the on-guard position, (2) quickly step forward three to four inches with the front foot. (3) Quickly slide the rear foot forward to replace the front and simultaneously lift the front foot to kick. (4) Deliver a hook kick to the opponent's midsection.

**Jeet Kune Do
Pendulum Steps**

(1) From the on-guard position, (2) shuffle the front foot backward. (3) At the same time, let the rear foot swing backward. The entire weight should rest on the front foot with the rear foot touching slightly for good balance. Immediately thereafter, shuffle the rear foot forward to regain the distance with the option to kick or back to on-guard position.

Application of the Jeet Kune Do Pendulum Steps

(1) From the on-guard position, (2) the defender uses the pendulum step to back away as an opponent attempts a side kick. As the opponent completes the side kick, the defender immediately swings the rear foot forward to regain the distance.

Chapter 2

HAND TECHNIQUES

The wing chun straight punch and the jeet kune do straight punch would at first appear similar, but the differences between them reveal some of the basic differences in the approach to generating power. Both profess the vertical fist, and keeping the elbow in to generate force from the center of the body. However, wing chun advises the independent movment of the arm and the shoulders, and, to stay balanced, not overreaching. Footwork is used to establish a close enough distance. Jeet kune do, on the other hand, advises putting the shoulders into the punch, and even reaching upon impact, the sideward stance, compensating one's balance. Jeet kune do also is capable of initiating the straight punch from farther out.

Wing Chun Straight Punch

The wing chun straight punch is usually performed with the lead hand, the rear hand being positioned for primarily defensive purposes. This is the basis of the jeet

kune do on-guard position. (1) To execute the wing chun straight punch, place the rear hand close to the lead elbow to protect the centerline. (2) Punch with the lead fist, keeping it positioned vertically, and striking with the lower three knuckles. Use your rear hand to parry the opponent's technique.

Jeet Kune Do Straight Punch

(1) From the on-guard position, (2) lead off the front hand from the center of your body in the form of a vertical fist. Punch straight ahead. Put your shoulder into the blow for added power and reach at impact.

Wing Chun Lead Punch to the Body

Landing a straight punch to body usually assumes having to parry and come under the opponent's technique. (1) From a neutral side stance, (2) step forward into a front stance, crouch under the opponent's technique as you parry it to the outside, and execute the straight punch to the ribs.

Jeet Kune Do Lead Punch to the Body

(1) From the on-guard position, (2) deliver the lead punch by dropping the body forward as you step in, sinking the lead shoulder to the target level as you shoot out the lead punch.

1

Wing Chun
Rear Hand Strike

Though the rear hand is usually positioned defensively, it is often used to strike. However, usually when it is used for striking, the risk of the extra distance it must travel is secured by using the front hand to inhibit the opponent's ability to counter. (1) Establishing contact, (2) parry the opponent's technique and trap his forward elbow by pinning it to his body. This (3) turns his body, and allows you to land the rear hand strike. Even with the rear hand strike it should be noted that the force of the punch is directed forward from the center, independent of the shoulders. The body is not twisted.

2

3

Jeet Kune Do
Straight Rear Cross

(1) From the on-guard position, (2) rotate the hip clockwise by pivoting the the rear foot. As you pivot, drive the rear fist straight out in front of your nose. Your weight shifts forward into the punch to your lead foot.

Wing Chun Palm Strike

There are several types of wing chun palm strike, the straight palm strike wtih the fingers angled upward, the reverse palm strike in which the fingers angle downward, and the double palm strike with one hand executing straight palm strike and the other executing reverse palm strike. (1) From a neutral side stance, be sure to keep the rear hand close to the front elbow to protect the centerline. (2) Use the rear hand to control the opponent's technique, and (3) strike directly forward with the palm of the front hand.

Jeet Kune Do Palm Hook

Jeet kune do prefers to use a hooking motion in delivering the palm strike rather than the straight ahead motion of wing chun. (1) From the on-guard position, (2) use the rear hand to control the opponent's technique just as in the wing chun example, except to execute the palm strike, extend the lead arm completely, whip it out in a full arc toward the target. As you rotate the hip and the shoulder, use the heel of the palm as the contact surface.

1

2

Wing Chun Finger Jab

There are four types of wing chun finger jabs as the fingers may be angled vertically up or down, or laterally inside or outside. (1) From a neutral side stance, (2) execute the outward finger jab by positioning your palm laterally, and angling your fingers outward as you strike with the tips of your fingers to the eyes of the opponent.

Jeet Kune Do Finger Jab

(1) From the on-guard position, (2) whip the lead arm straight out with the fingers extended. This technique applies the shocking, flicking force rather than the punching force.

1

2

Wing Chun Elbow Strike

In executing elbow strikes, wing chun prefers, but does not always support, the striking arm by placing the palm of the other hand over the fist of the striking arm. (1) To execute the backward elbow strike against an opponent who is behind, (2) bring the arms forward to loosen his hold and gain more striking room. (3) Strike by driving the elbow backward into the opponent's abdomen, using the other hand to support the striking arm.

Jeet Kune Do Elbow Strike

Jeet kune do also uses a variety of elbow strikes, but chooses to enhance power with the backward elbow strike. (1) The jeet kune do backward elbow strike is also used primarily to counter a grab from behind. (2) To execute the elbow stirke, step back with the foot of the same side as the striking elbow. Extra momentum is gained by this slight rotation of the body into the strike rather than from a supporting hand.

Wing Chun Larp Sao

(1&2) As the opponent punches, parry his arm to the outside, by circling your wrist inward. (3) Grab and pull his arm as you simultaneously step diagonally forward, and (4) land an elbow strike to the ribs.

Jeet Kune Do Larp Sao

(1) From the cross hand position, (2) grab and pull the opponent's wrist. (3) Follow with a rear hand straight punch to the head.

Wing Chun Tsuen Sao

The wing chun tsuen sao is comparable to jeet kune do's jao sao. Both involve an initial strike which is parried by the opponent. The striking hand is then withdrawn, and another strike is attempted with that same hand through a different opening. The non-striking hand is used to execute a trap on the opponent's arm just as the initial strike is blocked. The trap is maintained as the second strike is executed. To execute tsuen sao, (1&2) initiate a strike which the opponent blocks or parries. With the rear hand placed under the elbow of the striking hand, slide the rear hand upward under the striking forearm and (3) engage the opponent's arm as your striking arm withdraws. (4) Execute another strike with the striking arm as you maintain the check on the opponent's arm.

Jeet Kune Do Jao Sao

(1) From the cross hand position, (2) disengage the front hand, and trap with the rear hand. (3) Follow with a palm strke to the head.

Wing Chun Pak Sao

The wing chun pak sao and the jeet kune do pak sao are identical, except for the follow-up footwork to land the counter. In both, the pak sao and counter are in rapid combination, practiced almost as one movement. (1) To execute pak sao, use the rear hand to slap the opponent's technique to the opposite side, and (2) follow instantly with a counter.

Jeet Kune Do Pak Sao

(1) From the cross hand position, (2) immobilize the opponent's arm with a slapping rear hand, then (3) follow through with a front hand punch to the ribs.

Wing Chun Jut Sao

Both the wing chun jut sao and the jeet kune do jut sao use a downward pushing movement to clear the path for a counter. This push is very often quite forceful. In wing chun, however, the heel of the palm is used to push down while the hand remains open. (1) In this example, a double jut sao is used to pull down both of the opponent's arms. Then (2) one forearm is used to trap across both the opponent's forearms. This frees the other hand to land a punch to the face.

Jeet Kune Do Jut Sao

(1) In jeet kune do, double jut sao is executed by grabbing both the opponent's wrists with both hands, (2) pulling them down, and trapping with one forearm in order to free the other hand for (3) a counter to the head.

Wing Chun Back Fist

The wing chun back fist is delivered, as with most wing chun strikes, on a straight line, the elbow tucked close to the center, and the fist turned so the back of the hand faces the target. The back of the kunckles is the contact point. (1-3) The opponent's techniques are parried until (4) an opening occurs, and as the back fist is connected, the fist is driven straight forward to the target.

Jeet Kune Do Back Fist

(1) From the on-guard position, the opponent's technique is parried, and his arms are trapped. (2) The back fist is delivered by whipping the lead arm out in a horizontal semicircular motion. The body weight is shifted to the front and the back of the knuckles is used as the contact point.

Wing Chun Side Attack

(1) In order to attack the opponent from the side, wing chun (2) uses footwork to step to the opponent's outside, trapping the elbow to turn the opponent further, and striking to a side target such as the ribs.

Jeet Kune Do Hook Punch

(1) Attacking from the side, jeet kune do tries to come around the opponent's defenses by using the hook punch. From the on-guard position, (2) deliver the hook punch by whipping the lead arm forward in an arc toward the target, keeping the rear guard high. Keep the arm tight, and rotate the lead hip and lead shoulder into the punch, shifting weight to the rear foot as you drive the hook through the target.

Wing Chun Gum Sao

(1&2) As the opponent attempts a kick, (3) step back to gain some distance, and execute gum sao by pushing the lead palm down to block the kick.

Jeet Kune Do Gum Sao

The jeet kune do gum sao is also usually used to block kicks. (1&2) As the opponent attempts a kick, (3) skip backward to gain some distance, and execute gum sao to block the kick.

Chapter 3

KICKING

Because wing chun uses three different stances, it may appear that there are various ways of executing the same kick. For example, the procedure for throwing a front kick from a neutral side stance appears different from the procedure involved in throwing a front kick from a front stance, etc. However, there is only one simple rule to follow: the kicking foot, wherever it happens to be positioned, to the front, to the side, or to the rear, must be pulled through the center before being snapped or thrust into the kicking motion.

In jeet kune do, on the other hand, because there is only one basic stance, and because the lead leg is favored in the execution of offensive techniques, the techniques used in kicking are fewer and simpler. Jeet kune do also prefers a more direct line to the target and generally ignores pulling the kicking foot through the center before executing the kick. The kicking foot is usually aimed toward the target directly from its original position.

Another major difference between wing chun kicks and jeet kune do kicks is that in most jeet kune do kicks, some forward movement is initiated before the kicking action. The lead foot slides forward then the rear foot skips up and supplants the forward foot which is simultaneously raised to execute the kick.

The kick, which wing chun refers to as "round kick," that is executed with a swinging movement of the leg in an arc from the outside inward, is also part of the jeet kune do arsenal, except that jeet kune do calls it "hook kick."

There are two jeet kune do side kicks shown. The reason for making the distinction between the high side kick and the low side kick is not just a difference in target area, but a difference also in purpose. The low side kick is also referred to as a stop kick, indicating its use as a defensive technique, or as a pre-emptive strike to obstruct the opponent's ability to kick. Wing chun's reverse side kick serves a comparable purpose.

Wing chun's reverse side kick is juxtaposed to the jeet kune do reverse hook kick in way of comparison only because of the inside out movement that is involved in both. However, the wing chun reverse hook kick serves a pre-emptive or defensive purpose whereas the jeet kune do reverse hook kick is a decidedly offensive tool.

The last two kicks shown in this chapter, the wing chun stomp kick and the jeet kune do spin kick, are not meant to be compared. These are two totally different kicks that really have nothing in common except that they are both important as major techniques in their respective arts, and neither appears to have any counterpart in the other's arsenal.

Wing Chun Front Kick

(1) Commence on a right neutral side stance. (2) Execute a right bil sao. (3) Bring your right foot across close to the left foot. (4) Execute a front kick with the right foot. (5) Step forward with the right foot to form a right front stance.

1

3

5

Jeet Kune Do Front Kick

(1) From the on-guard position, (2) take a quick step forward with the lead foot about three to four inches. (3) Immediately slide the rear foot forward to replace the front foot, and (4) simultaneously lift the front foot to kick. (5) Deliver the kick straight toward the target using the ball of the foot as the contact surface.

1

3

5

Wing Chun Side Kick

(1) Commence on a right neutral side stance. (2) Bring the right foot across close to the left foot. (3) Bring the left knee up. (4) Execute a low side kick. (5) Step forward to form a right front stance.

1

3

5

Jeet Kune Do Side Kick

(1) From the on-guard position, (2) quick-step forward three to four inches with the lead foot. (3) Immediately slide the rear foot forward to replace the lead foot. (4) Simultaneously lift the lead foot high to deliver the side kick. (5) Straighten both legs out at the moment of impact.

1

3

Jeet Kune Do Low Side Kick or Stop Kick

(1) From the on-guard position, (2) slide the rear foot forward quickly to replace the front foot and simultaneously lift the front foot. (3) Immediately deliver the kick in a diagonally downward direction to the opponent's knee or shin.

1

2

5

3

Wing Chun Round Kick

(1) Commence on a right neutral side stance. (2) Bring the right knee up. (3) Execute a round kick. (4) Step forward and (5) form a front stance.

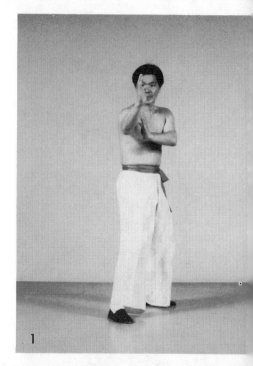

1

3

5

Jeet Kune Do Hook (Round) Kick

(1) From the on-guard position, (2) quick-step forward three to four inches with the front foot. (3) Immediately slide the rear foot forward to replace the front foot. (4) Simultaneously lift the front foot high to kick. (5) Deliver the kick to the target. The hook kick travels in a semi-circular path and uses the instep or shin as the contact surface.

1

3

5

Wing Chun
Reverse Side Kick

(1) Commence on a right neutral side stance. (2) Execute a tan sao and palm strike, and at the same time, lift the right knee up, and execute a reverse side kick by turning the foot outward and stomping forward. (3) Step down into a right neutral side stance.

Jeet Kune Do
Reverse Hook Kick

(1) From the on-guard position, (2) quickstep forward three to four inches with the lead foot. Immediately slide the rear foot forward to replace the lead foot, and simultaneously lift the lead leg up to kick. (3) The kick is delivered outward. Using the right foot, the kick arcs from left to right. The outside edge of the foot is the contact surface.

Wing Chun Stomp Kick

(1) Commence on a right neutral side stance. (2) Execute a double larp sao, and at the same time bring the knee up. (3). Execute a stomp kick. (4) Step forward to form a right front stance.

Jeet Kune Do Spin Kick

(1) From the on-guard position, (2) lift the rear leg and bring it close to the lead leg which now becomes the pivot leg. (3) Quickly pivot the body 180 degrees. If the pivot leg is the right leg, the left leg would be the kicking leg, and the pivot would be counterclockwise. (4) Thrust the kicking foot straight out to deliver the kick.

Chapter 4

TACTICS

This chapter compares some of wing chun's and jeet kune do's basic tactics. First, the distinction between traditional wing chun and modified wing chun is drawn to clarify some of the reasons why Bruce Lee decided that the shortcomings of the wing chun he learned, modified wing chun, rendered that method insufficient in dealing with certain aspects of real combat.

The basis of their respective tactics is also examined. While wing chun stresses ambidexterity, jeet kune do prefers to put the strong side forward. From these basic decisions, other tactics regarding how to gain the advantage, and how to bridge the gap derive their similarities and differences.

Comparing Traditional Wing Chun,
Modified Wing Chun, and Jeet Kune Do

It is important in comparing wing chun and jeet kune do to understand some of the reasons Bruce Lee felt it necessary to experiment with new methods and eventually establish jeet kune do.

Some of the technical reasons have to do with the failures of the modified wing chun method he was taught. In this modified wing chun system, the practitioner is taught to face his opponent centerline to centerline. The centerline is an imaginary vertical line "drawn" along the center of the body, dividing the body vertically into two halves. Most of the body's vital targets are located on the centerline. Thus in modified wing chun, the opponent's centerline is used as the main focus of offense and protecting one's own centerline is the main concern of defensive techniques.

* *Centerline*

Traditional wing chun professes the use of the central line. According to this prescription the practitioner does not necessarily face the opponent centerline to centerline, a tactic which promotes primarily frontal attacks and defenses. Traditional wing chun uses footwork to keep and maneuver the opponent within an area rather than on a line. Techniques are often executed at angles off the centerline but within the central line area. Sidestepping with a T-stance, followed by a diagonal forward step is typical in traditional wing chun. Modified wing chun does not use the T-stance, a maueuver which allows the practitoner much more lateral mobility. This means being able to cut off much of the opponent's lateral movements more effeciently.

The central line, the crux of traditional wing chun, enables the practitioner to use two arms at the same time. Striking from the center minimizes the striking distance and shortens the time for coming back to the defense position, while the elbow is used to protect the target area.

The centerline is a vertical imaginary line, "drawn" along the center of the body, dividing the body vertically into two halves. Most of the body's vital targets are located on the centerline.

A

Focus Areas of the Central Line

The central line focuses technique within an area (A-D) defined by where the practitioner is able to cross both wrists out in front of his body without having to pivot. (E&F) Where the wrists are unable to cross without turning the body is considered outside the central line area. If an opponent ends up at such an angle relative to the practitioner, footwork is used to make adjustments.

D

Outside the Focus Area

These angles (A&B) are outside the central line focus area. If the opponent ends up at such angles, footwork is used to bring him within the area.

A

1

Example of Failure of Modified Wing Chun

One failure of modifed wing chun is a lack of structural strength in sideward directions. In this example (1&2) the practitioner faces the opponent's centerline. However, a forceful round punch (3) collapses the block and manages to land. Note that much of the stress on the blocking arm is from left to right, whereas the structural strength of the block is directed forward, toward the opponent's centerline. Only the muscle power of the left shoulder supports this block in the outward direction, and it is not enough.

2

3

Example of the Advantage of Traditional Wing Chun's Central Line

(1) In this example, the practitioner is able to produce two independent lines of force, both simultaneously supported by structural strength. (2&3) The opponent throws a round punch. The practitioner steps diagonally to angle the structural strength of his block outward, and (4) at the same time lands a counter along another line. Both the block and the counter are structurally supported. By keeping his elbows in, power is generated from the center.

Example of Jeet Kune Do Solution

The type of block used in modified and traditional wing chun (tan sao) is not used in jeet kune do. Jeet kune do uses a technique of parrying which according to its philosophy is a simple, more instictive movement. In this example, the round punch is (1&2) blocked agressively before it reaches full extension. Structurally it can be seen that the line of the upper arm opposes the direction of the blow almost directly. (3) The same arm is then used to follow through with a counter, the body swinging from left to right to generate power.

Basis of Technique

• *Wing Chun's Ambidexterous Approach*

In wing chun, the practitoner is taught to practice techniques on both sides, as well as to develop the ability to move them independently of the shoulders. Using the type of footwork which often switches lead sides from right to left and vice versa, being able to execute all techniques ambidexterously is vital to being effective in wing chun. The *shil lim tao* form is especially designed to develop the ability to move the arms independently of the shoulders. Both these abilities allow the wing chun practitioner to simultaneously block with one hand and counter with the other.

• *Jeet Kune Do's Strong Side Forward Approach*

In jeet kune do, 80 percent of all striking is done with the lead hand or foot. Therefore, jeet kune do teaches to put the strong side forward. This makes jeet kune do structurally fast. If the right hand is stronger, and has more endurance, speed, and coordination, it should be used the most. In this case then, the strongest weapon is thrown across the shortest distance, minimizing the opponent's chance of reacting to the attack.

But if the strong side is in the rear position, then the practitioner will be structurally slow, because although he will attempt to strike with it most of the time, it will have a longer distance to travel, and he will always telegraph his motion.The practitioner will also expose his centerline and groin with a rear weapon attack. Every time he strikes with the rear hand or rear foot, the whole front of his body is exposed, leaving very vulnerable targets open to the opponent. Also, because the left hand is weaker, it needs the extra distance and the swinging of the body to accumulate speed and power.

Gaining the Advantage: Wing Chun

• *Wing Chun's Golden Rule of Foot Placement*

To gain the advantage in combat, it is fundamental and essential that the practitioner attempt to place his lead foot in a very specific place in relation to his and his opponent's stance. In a parallel leg situation, that is when the practitioner's and the opponent's lead legs face each other, such as when the practitioner has his left leg in the lead and the opponent faces him with his right leg in the lead, wing chun recommends that the practitioner attempts to place his lead foot to the outside of the opponent's. And in a cross leg situation such as when the practitioner has his left leg in the lead and the opponent has his left leg in the lead, wing chun recommends placing the lead foot to the inside of the opponent's.

Another of wing chun's fundamental tactics in gaining the advantage is the use of the neutral side stance.

**Parallel Leg Situation:
Correct Foot Placement**

(1) The practitioner commences in a right neutral side stance. (2) The attacker steps in with a right punch, but the defender deflects it with a left pak sao and at the same time steps forward with the left foot and places it just outside the attacker's right foot. The defender then executes a right punch to the attacker's body.

Parallel Leg Situation: Incorrect Foot Placement

(1) If the practitioner steps with the his left lead foot inside the attacker's right lead foot, his right fist would not have reached the attacker at all. (2) The attacker could also easily push the practitioner off balance, or (3) sweep the practitioner with his right foot and turn the defender completely around helplessly.

Cross Leg Situation: Correct Foot Placement

(1) The practitioner commences with a right neutral side stance, and the attacker is in a right front stance. (2) The attacker steps in with a right punch, and the defender defelcts it with a left pak sao, and at the same time, the defender steps forward with the right foot, placing it inside the attacker's front foot and the defender punches to the attacker's body with his right fist.

Cross Leg Situation: Incorrect Foot Placement

(1) If the practitioner places his front foot outside his opponent's front foot, then (2) It is quite easy for the opponent to turn the defender around, so that the defender would be facing the opponent with his back, rendering him defenseless.

The Advantage of Using the Neutral Side Stance

The neutral stance should have the weight evenly distributed on both legs. (1) In the right neutral side stance, the right arm is in the lead facing the target, with the right foot also pointing toward the target. (2) As the opponent steps in with a right punch, the defender uses a left pak sao to deflect it, and at the same time, kicks to the opponent's body.

Gaining the Advantage: Jeet Kune Do

While wing chun attempts to gain an edge on the opponent through foot placement and positioning, jeet kune do does it moving in and out, by varying its attacks, and by being unpredictable. Jeet kune do uses five basic ways of attack in addition to combinations of these five ways. Jeet kune do makes great use of deception, feinting, and changing lines, and keeping the opponent on the defensive.

- *Jeet Kune Do's Five Ways of Attack*

1. SDA (Single Direct Attack)

A direct attack is composed of a single movement. The objective is to go to the target by the most direct route. Although it is the simplest of the attacks, it is the hardest to complete successfully because the speed and timing, as well as the penetration of the opponent's defenses must all be perfect.

A single direct attack is made into the line of engagement or into the opposite line by simply beating the opponent to the punch, or by catching him in a moment of vulnerability. When executing a single direct attack, you lunge to hit the opponent before he can parry, without any attempt to disguise the direction of the attack. Here, you would most likely use your longest weapon to the closest target.

When striking with the lead hand, it is advisable to constantly vary the position of your head for added protection against your opponent's counter. Keep the lead hand moving, as it not only keeps your opponent on the edge, but also can be delivered faster from motion than from a stationary postition. Also, to mimimize counters from the opponent, you should at times feint before leading. However, do not overdo the feinting or headwork. Remember simplicity.

Such an attack can also be thrown at an unexpected angle, sometimes preceded by a feint. This is called a Single Angular Attack (SAA). It is done by positioning your body in relation to the opponent so that an opening results. The judgment of distance must be good. Sidestepping or some kind of larteral movement is often used in this attack.

1

Examples of Single Direct Attack

(1) From the on-guard position, the defender (2) executes a pre-emptive finger jab to the eyes. The success of SDA depends on speed and catching the opponent off-guard. From the on-guard position (1a&2a) execute a side kick to mid-section. From the on-guard position (1b&2b) execute a side kick to the knee.

1a

1b

2. ABC (Attack By Combination)

ABC is a series of thrusts that follow each other naturally and are generally thrown to more than one line. ABC is generally composed of set-ups to maneuver the opponent into such a position or create such an opening that the final blow of the series will find a vulnerable spot. You want to make sure that your attacks are aggressive enough to get your opponent to back away, otherwise he may smother your attack combinations.

Example of Attack by Combination

(1) From the on-guard position, (2) the defender initiates a front hand lead to the head. (3) He continues with a rear cross to the head, (4) follows with a lead hook to the head, and (5) finishes with a hook kick to the midsection.

2

4

5

3. HIA (Hand Immobilization Attack)

HIA applies an immobilizing technique (trap) on the opponent's hand or leg, or head (by grabbing the hair) as you crash the line of engagement. Immobilization attacks can best be set up by using any of the other four ways of attack, and traps can be performed in combination or singularly.

You use this when there is a barrier, such as the opponent's arm, that prevents your weapon from scoring, or when you want the added protection of covering a threatening weapon such as a nearby fist when slipping or countering. Trapping keeps the opponent from moving that part of his body, offering you a safety zone from which to strike. It can also be used to force an opening: upon finding your opponent covered, you would attack his hand with sufficient force and vigor to turn it aside and make an opening for your hand on the lunge. Deflecting or trapping the hand while stepping forward, also limits the possibility of a successful jam from the opponent. Obstructing the leg as a preliminary step is likewise very effective.

Example of Hand Immobilization Attack

(1) From the on-guard position, the defender (2) bridges the gap with a leg obstruction,

1

and (3) follows with a pak sao and a lead punch to the head at the same time.

4. PIA (Progressive Indirect Attack)

A PIA begins with a feint or an uncommitted thrust designed to misdirect the opponent's reactions in order to open a line for the real attack which follows instantly. The principal use of the PIA is to overcome an opponent whose defense is strong enough and fast enough to deal with HIA and SDA. It is also used to offer variation to one's pattern of attack.

Example of Progressive Indirect Attack

(1) From the on-guard position, (2) the defender initiates a low punch to draw the opponent's block, then (3) continues with

The distance has to be closed up a good half by the feint. The feint should induce the opponent to think you are going to hit him in a particualr line; so it must be long enough to provoke a reaction. When the opponent moves his hand or arm to cover that line, another line will open and the real thrust strikes there. The succession of feint and real attack in PIA is executed in a single, forward motion. In this, it is distinctly unlike a SDA preceded by a feint, which would be two separate movements.

a high line attack and (4) finishes the opponent with a hook kick to the midsection.

5. ABD (Attack By Drawing)

This is a counterattack initiated by luring an opponent into committing to a move. You must induce the opponent to step forward in tempo into the "within distance" area, for instance, by leaving an apparent opening. Then you time his attack, and nail him while he is stepping forward, or merely shifting his weight forward, or when he shows any sign of heaviness, mentally or physically. The success of this attack largely depends on concealing your real intentions.

Or you could execute movements that he may try to time and counter in some manner such as a jam which you can predict with some moderate certainty. His commitment will not allow him to change his position or guard swiftly enough to deal successfully with your offense after his technique is parried.

Example of Attack by Drawing

(1) From the on-guard position, (2) the defender drops his lead hand to draw the opponent's front hand attack. (3) The defender then slips to the outside while the opponent is attacking and lands a rear cross to the midsection. (4) He then follows up with a front uppercut to the side, and (5) finishes with a rear palm strike to the face.

Bridging the Gap: Wing Chun

The wing chun entry technique bridges the gap from what wing chun refers to as the "before contact stage" to the "contact" and "exchange stages." These stages can be compared in terms of distance to jeet kune do's "kicking range" and "punching and trapping ranges" respectively. Similarly, the aim of jeet kune do's entry technique is to bridge the gap from the kicking range to the punching and trapping ranges.

Wing chun's entry technique uses a skip forward with the rear leg comparable to jeet kune do's skip with the rear leg from the edge of the kicking range. Both are used to close the distance. This is coupled with raising the forward knee to protect the lower body and a bil sao hand technique to engage the opponent. This use of the bil sao is comparable to jeet kune do's "asking hand" executed as part of its entry.

Upon landing, wing chun tries to gain the advantage by placing the forward foot to the outside in a parallel leg situation, and on the inside in a cross leg situation.

Jeet kune do's entry bridges the gap with a kicking technique which also includes a forward skip with the rear leg to close the distance. This is followed by the asking hand whose purpose is comparable to wing chun's bil sao technique which accompanies its forward skip—to engage the opponent.

Instead of guarding the lower body by raising the forward leg, jeet kune do uses a long range leg obstruction to pre-empt any kicks, and upon closing the gap, uses the asking hand to pre-empt any hand technique by the opponent.

So, while wing chun executes the forward skip and the low (raised front knee) and high (bil sao) guards simultaneously, jeet kune do executes first the forward skip and low guard (long- range pre-emptive leg obstruction), then as the range closes into the punching and trapping and infighting ranges, the asking hand is used.

- *Wing Chun Entry Technique*

The correct way to execute the wing chun entry technique is to use the leading leg as a shield for the middle and lower gates of the body so that you do not need to divert your attack to defense when you reach the opponent. The entry technique can be made from any stance, and any leg can become the lead leg. However, if that leg starts out from the rear, or from the side, it must be drawn through the center on its way up the shielding postion.

After bringing the front knee up to make a shield, you propel your body diagonally forward by pushing off with your supporting leg. Nevertheless, you must have perfect control of your balance once you achieve the contact stage. You do this by slowing down so that you are able to interrupt your movements if required. The arm of the leading side of the body accompanies this movement in the bil sao position.

Entry Technique: Example 1

(1) The practitioner is in a right neutral side stance, and the opponent is in a right front stance. (2) The practitioner executes the entry technique, and the opponent uses his right foot to jam his front leg. (3) The practitioner withdraws his right leg, and brings it around, placing it inside the opponent's leg, and simultaneously traps the opponent's right arm. (4) The practitioner then follows up with a left punch to the opponent's face.

Entry Technique: Example 2

(1) The practitioner is in a right neutral side stance, and the opponent is in a right front stance. (2) The practitioner executes the entry technique, and the opponent steps back with his right foot. (3) As the opponent shoots out a left

punch, the practitioner deflects it with his right bil sao, and kicks to the opponent's body. (4) The practitioner lands with his front foot outside the opponent's left foot, and punches with his left fist to the opponent's face.

**Entry Technique:
Example 3**

(1) The practitioner is in a left neutral side stance, and the opponent is in a right front stance. (2&3) The practitioner executes a left entry technique. The opponent punches with his right arm, and the

practitioner uses a left pak sao to deflect it. (4) The practitioner places his left foot outside the opponent's right foot, and punches with his right fist to the face.

**Entry Technique:
Example 4**

(1) The practitioner is in a left neutral side stance, and the opponent is in a right front stance. (2&3) The practitioner executes the entry technique, and the opponent steps back with his rear foot. (4) As soon as the practitioner lands with

his left foot, he follows through with a right front kick to the opponent's body. (5) He places his right foot to the inside of the opponent's right foot, checks the right elbow, and punches to the face.

Entry Technique:
Example 5

(1) The practitioner is in a left neutral side stance, and the opponent is in a right front stance. (2-4) As the practitioner executes a left entry, the opponent steps back. (5&6) The practitioner immediately executes a second left entry. (7) As the practitioner lands with his left foot outside the opponent's right foot, the opponent punches with his right arm, and the practitioner deflects it with a left pak sao. (8) The practitioner then follows up by checking the opponent's right arm, and lands a punch to the face.

5

8

Entry Technique:
Example 6

(1) The practitoner is in a right neutral side stance, and the opponent is in a right front stance. (2-4) As the practitioner executes a right entry, the opponent steps back. (5&6) The practitioner immediately executes a second entry technique to catch up with the opponent. (7) He follows up with a left punch to the face while his left hand maintains a check on the opponent's right arm.

3

6

5

Entry Technique:
Example 7

(1) The practitioner is in a right neutral side stance, and the opponent is in a right front stance. (2-4) The practitioner executes a right entry, and the opponent steps backward with his left foot. (5) As a result, the practitioner lands with still a considerable distance between him and the opponent. (6) The practitioner then executes a left round kick to the opponent's right thigh. (7) He then lands with his left foot outside of the opponent's right foot and punches to the face with his right fist while his left hand maintains a check on the opponent's right elbow.

5

Bridging the Gap: Jeet Kune Do

Wing chun and jeet kune do consider the gap in different ways. Jeet kune do considers the gap as a distance that is carefully judged and maintained. In jeet kune do, the gap should be of such a distance that your opponent cannot hit you unless he lunges fully at you, but not so far that with a short advance you cannot regain your own effective range and be able to reach him with your own powerful attack. Your fighting distance depends on your opponent's reach and speed as well as your own. In jeet kune do the art of successful kicking and hitting is the art of correct distance judging, of controlling the fighting distance, and bridging it with speed and agility when attacking.

The jeet kune do fighter is constantly gaining and breaking ground, trying to make the opponent misjudge his distance while he remains well aware of his own.

In bridging the gap, you want to catch your opponent in an unprepared state of mind. The opponent should be lulled, then the attack should be launched as suddenly as possible. An attack should be aimed at the distance where the opponent will be when he realizes he is being attacked and not at the distance prior to the attack. Make sure to immobilize your opponent's leg when getting close.

Sometimes it is best to let the opponent bridge the gap by allowing him to attack, then counter his movement. This is a strategy that you use against a fighter who never allows you to get close enough to hit him. You control the distance for countering, without allowing your opponent to bridge the gap unless you want him to, and are prepared to counter him.

You must also be aware of the "no man's land." This is the space in which you and your opponent are so close that you have no chance of defending against his attack. This area can be very long or short, depending on your reaction speed and the speed of your opponent. You want to be on the brim of this line but no closer. Once you cross this line, or the opponent crosses this line, you should either re-adjust the distance, or attack, or be prepared for his attack, otherwise you will most likely be dealing with an attack you have little chance of defending successfully.

Bridging the Gap: Example 1

(1) From the on-guard position, (2) the practitioner executes a leg obstruction to bridge the gap. (3) He then executes a hand technique which the opponent must parry. This is known as the asking hand, which gets the practitioner into the cross hand position. (4) The practitioner follows with a pak sao and punch. (5) When the opponent cross blocks the punch, the practitioner follows with a rear hand larp sao counter. (6) Then he follows up with a front hand back fist to the face.

**Bridging the Gap:
Example 2**

(1) From the on-guard position, (2) the practitioner bridges the gap with a leg obstruction. (3) He then executes the asking hand to get into the cross hand position. (4) The practitioner then ex-

ecutes a larp sao and a rear punch to the head. (5) When the opponent blocks the punch with his rear hand, the practitioner counters with a rear hand larp sao and front hand punch to the face.

Bridging the Gap: Example 3

(1) From the on-guard position, (2) the practitioner bridges the gap with a leg obstruction. (3) He executes the asking hand to get into the cross hand position. (4) He then executes a pak sao and

low punch to the ribs. (5) When the opponent blocks the punch with his rear hand, the practitioner counters with a jull sao and palm strike to the side of the head.

Bridging the Gap: Example 4

(1) From the on-guard position, (2) the practitioner bridges the gap with a leg obstruction. (3) He executes the asking hand, (4) follows with a pak sao and low punch to the ribs. When the opponent blocks the punch, the practitioner (5) follows with another pak sao, and (6) a punch to the head. (7) When the opponent bocks that punch, the practitioner counters with a larp sao, and follows with (8) a hook kick to the ribs.

2

4

5

7

8

Bridging the Gap: Example 5

(1) From the on-guard position, (2) the practitioner bridges the gap with a leg obstruction. (3) He executes the asking hand. (4) He disengages the front hand and traps with the rear hand, and (5) follows with a palm hook to the head. (6) When the opponent blocks the palm hook, the practitioner grabs both wrists, (7) jerks them downward, and (8) follows with a pushing arm block over both arms. He disengages the front hand, and (9) lands a vertical palm strike to the head.

Chapter 5

SELF-DEFENSE

This chapter presents examples of self-defense situations which include empty-hand attacks, kicking attacks, knife attacks, club attacks, and staff attacks. It shows alternately how wing chun handles a particular self-defense situation, and then how jeet kune do handles the same situation. In this way, the reader may compare strategies and techniques, and the general character of both arts.

It can be seen for example how the more complex stances and footwork of wing chun manifest themselves in combat as an emphasis on stability, rootedness, and standing balance from which the power of the techniques is derived. In the wing chun front punch, the feet remain planted, so the punch is structurally supported by a strong foundation. Whereas in jeet kune do, the emphasis is on momentum, and the dynamics of the body in motion. The power of the jeet kune do lead punch comes from a whip-like accumulation of speeds of all segments of the body from the toes of the rear leg pushing off, upward, and culminating in the fist. Thus in jeet kune do, the rear heel is raised with the rear foot already in position to provide leverage to propel the body forward. And upon impact, it is the momentum of the whole body that drives the punch. Thus, in these wing chun examples of self-defense, the body can be observed to be more upright under all conditions and all stages of combat, but in the jeet kune do examples, the body is usually crouched at the beginning and then fully extended and leaning forward into the technique at the end.

Wing chun's more ambidexterous approach is also evident in how the defender "walks" his way in from the parry, to the trap, to the finishing blow, while jeet kune do's theory of the strong side forward, and simultaneous parry and counter, results in slightly longer steps in order to close the distance as rapidly as possible. It is also evident that jeet kune do incorporates more throwing techniques and leg sweeps than wing chun.

Still, the reader will observe many similarities in technique between wing chun's handling of a situation, and jeet kune do's handling of the same circumstance. As an example, one of jeet kune do's methods of breaking a wrist grab with a downward chopping motion of the other hand, is actually one of the last movements in wing chun's *sil lim tao* formal exercise, underscoring the technical relatedness of the two arts.

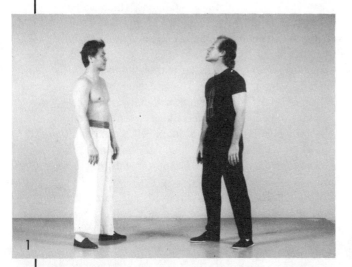

Wing Chun Against a Grab to the Throat

(1) The attacker and defender are standing facing each other. (2) The attacker reaches for the defender's throat, but the defender uses a left *pak sao* to deflect his hand. (3&4) The defender then uses a right pak

3

sao to move the attacker's arm aside to his right. (5) The defender then grabs the attacker's arm, pulling the attacker's body down, and drives his right knee into the attacker's face.

4

5

Jeet Kune Do Against a Grab to the Throat

(1) The attacker and the defender stand facing each other. (2) The attacker reaches for the defender's throat. (3)

the defender parries the attack outward as he steps forward with his right foot, and (4) executes a finger jab to the eyes.

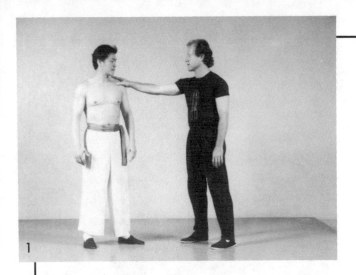

Wing Chun Against a Grab on the Shoulder

(1) The attacker grabs the defender on the shoulder with his right hand. (2) The defender turns sharply and applies a left larp sao on the attacker's right elbow, grabs the arm, then follows with a right side palm to the attacker's temple. (3) The defender then pulls the attacker's head down, and knees him to the face.

Jeet Kune Do Against a Grab on the Shoulder

(1) The attacker and defender stand facing each other. (2) The attacker attempts to control the defender by grabbing his shoulder. The defender steps forward with his strong side, and immobilizes the attacker's arm. Then (3) he executes a front punch to the head.

Wing Chun Against a Grab on the Shoulder From Behind

(1) The attacker grabs the defender on the shoulder from behind. (2) The defender steps forward with his left foot, turns around, pivoting to his right, and applies a right bil sao to the attacker's right arm. (3) The defender then kicks to the attacker's body, and while still holding the arm, follows up with a punch to the attacker's head.

Jeet Kune Do Against a Grab on the Shoulder From Behind

(1) The attacker approaches from behind, and grabs the defender's shoulders. (2) The defender executes a back kick to the attacker's groin to break his hold, then (3) follows with a side kick to the attacker's chest.

Wing Chun Against a Head Lock

(1) The attacker applies a head lock on the defender. (2) The defender turns his head around and at the same time applies a left elbow strike to the attacker's body, breaking his grip. (3) The defender then turns around, and lands a right palm strike to the attacker's jaw.

Jeet Kune Do Against a Rear Choke Hold

(1) The attacker approaches from behind and attempts a rear choke hold. The defender immediately reaches up with both hands to grab the choking arm. (2) The defender leans forward suddenly, and throws the attacker over his shoulder. (3) The defender then follows up with a kick to the head.

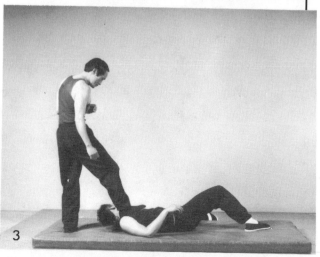

Wing Chun Against a Parallel Arm Wrist Grab

(1) The attacker uses his right arm to grab the defender's left wrist. (2) The defender uses a right palm against the attacker's right arm, at the same time pulling his left arm away. (3) The defender checks the attacker's right elbow with his left palm, and punches with his right fist to the attacker's temple.

Jeet Kune Do Against a Parallel Arm Wrist Grab

(1) The attacker and defender stand facing each other. (2) The attacker reaches and grabs the defender by the wrist. The defender rotates his hand upward on the inside to grab the attacker's wrist with a larp sao. He then pulls the attacker toward him, (3) steps forward with his strong side, and executes a punch to the head.

Wing Chun Against
a Parallel Arm Vertical Wrist Grab

(1) The attacker applies a right vertical grip to the defender's left wrist. (2) The defender applies a sudden jerk on the attacker's pressure point situated between the thumb and index finger knuckles, and (3) follows up with a punch to the attacker's head.

Jeet Kune Do Against
a Parallel Arm Vertical Wrist Grab

(1&2) The attacker grabs the defender's wrist, and the defender counters by grabbing the attacker's elbow. (3) The defender then pushes up on the elbow on the inside as he sweeps the wrist downward on the outside (4&5) for a leveraged throw.

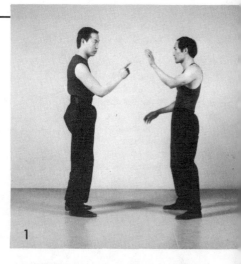

2

3

2

1

5

147

1

Wing Chun Against a Cross Arm Grip to the Wrist

(1) The attacker grabs the defender's wrist. (2) The defender turns the attacker's arm around, and (3) palms off the

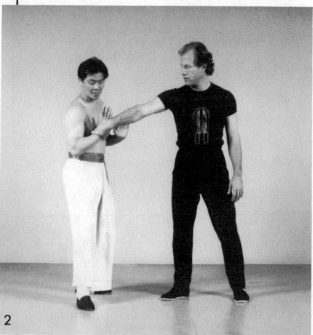

2

3

attacker's arm, and pulls his right arm away. (4) The defender then follows up with a punch to the attacker's head.

4

Jeet Kune Do Against a Cross Arm Wrist Grab

(1&2) The attacker reaches across and grabs the defender's wrist. (3) The defender breaks his hold with a downward chopping motion. (Note that this is also a wing

chun technique.) At the same time, (4) the defender also traps that arm, and (5) follows through with a front punch to the head.

Wing Chun Against a Straight Punch

(1) The defender is in a right neutral side stance. (2) The attacker steps in, strikes with the right fist, and the defender uses a left pak sao to deflect it. (3) The defender follows up with a right bil sao to push the

3

attacker's right arm across, then (4) steps forward with his right foot, and (5) executes a palm strike to the attacker's jaw, and throws him to the ground.

4

5

1

Jeet Kune Do Against a Straight Punch

(1&2) The attacker attempts a straight punch, and the defender steps to the outside. (3) The defender grabs the attacker's wrist with his rear hand, and places his lead arm across the attacker's chest. The defender pulls the

2

3

attacker's wrist in order to shift his weight to his forward leg. (4) The defender applies backward pressure to the attacker's chest as he blocks the defender's forward leg for (5) a takedown.

4

5

Wing Chun Neck and Shoulder Lock
Against a Straight Punch

(1) The defender is in a right neutral side stance. (2) The attacker steps in with a right fist. The defender uses a pak sao to deflect it and at the same time finger jabs to the body. (3) The defender steps around to the back of the attacker with his left foot, and at the same time brings his right arm underneath the attacker's right arm and around his neck. The defender then applies a neck and shoulder lock to disable the attacker.

Jeet Kune Do
Front Arm Choke Hold

(1) With the defender in the on-guard position, the opponent (2) throws a front hand punch. The defender (3) slips to the outside and applies a front arm choke hold. (4-6) He then positions his front leg behind the opponent's front leg and sweeps the opponent's front leg for the takedown.

3

3

6

Wing Chun Against
a Leading Front Kick

(1-3) As the attacker raises his leg to begin his motion for a front kick, the defender uses his lead leg to (4) jam the attacker's leg at the knee. (5) He then steps forward, placing his front foot inside the attacker's front foot, checks the attacker's right arm with his right hand, and executes a left punch to the attacker's face.

Jeet Kune Do Against
a Leading Front Kick

(1&2) As the attacker raises his leg to begin his front kick motion, the defender intercepts it with a low side stop kick to the shin. (3) The defender then steps forward with his strong side, and executes a front hand punch to his head.

5

3

Wing Chun Against a Round Kick: Example 1

(1) The attacker attempts a right round kick to the head. (2) The defender uses a right pak sao and left tan sao to block it. (3) The defender then moves up with a right fist to the face while his left hand checks the attacker's right arm.

Jeet Kune Do Against a Round Kick: Example 1

(1&2) As the attacker attempts a round kick, the defender intercepts it by executing a reverse hook kick to the inner thigh. (3) He then follows with a front hand punch to the head.

Wing Chun Against a Round Kick: Example 2

(1&2) The attacker moves in with a left round kick, and the defender (3) uses a right garn sao to block it. (4) The defender grabs the attacker's ankle with his right hand, while his left hand controls the knee,

and he drives his own right knee upward to execute a leg break. (5&6) The defender then moves up to check the defender's left elbow, and lands a right punch to his head.

Jeet Kune Do Against a Round Kick: Example 2

(1&2) When the attacker attempts a rear leg round kick, the defender steps forward and catches the leg before it

3

reaches full extension. The defender (3) steps forward with his own rear leg, and (4&5) sweeps the attacker's support leg.

4

5

Wing Chun Against a Straight Thrust

(1) The defender stands with his hands alongside his body as he faces the attacker who holds a knife in his right hand. (2) The attacker steps in with a straight thrust, and the defender uses a left pak sao to deflect it. The defender then puts his left thumb on the knuckle of the middle finger of the attacker's right hand, and the right thumb on top of his left thumb. (3) The defender then drops sharply to the ground, bringing the attacker to the ground.

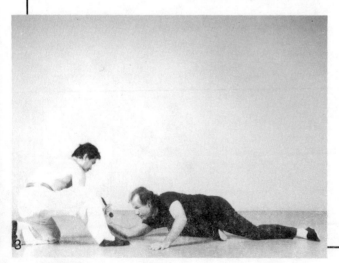

Jeet Kune Do Against a Straight Thrust

(1) The defender faces the attacker who has a knife. (2) The attacker attempts a straight thrust attack for the defender's midsection. The defender (3) evades the attack by sidestepping to the outside, and executing a reverse hook kick to the attacker's elbow.

Wing Chun Against a Round Slash

(1-3) The defender stands with his arms alongside his body. The attacker steps in with a right round slash, and the defender uses a right pak sao at the wrist to stop it. (4) The defender then pushes the attacker's arm upward and at

the same time steps across to the left. (5) The defender then places his left hand just behind the attacker's right elbow, pushing it down sharply to bring the attacker to his knees.

Jeet Kune Do Against a Round Slash

(1&2) The attacker attempts a slashing attack. (3) The defender evades the attack by retreating backwards. (4&5)

The defender then counters with a low side kick to the attacker's knee.

Wing Chun Against an Overhead Stab

(1-3) The defender stands with his arms alongside the body. The attacker steps in with an overhead stab, and the defender brings his right hand up to block it at the wrist. At the same time, he brings his

left hand behind the attacker's right arm and hooks it through in front of his forearm. (4) The defender then steps behind the attacker's right foot, and applies pressure to push the attacker off balance.

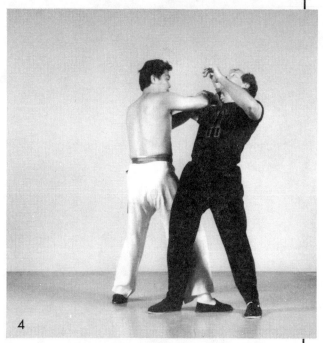

1

Jeet Kune Do Against an Overhead Stab

(1-3) As the attacker attempts an overhead stab at the defender, the defender intercepts and traps the attacker's upper arm with his rear hand. (4) The defender slips his front arm under the attacker's knife arm to grab the wrist while he

2

3

4

positions his front leg behind the attacker's front leg. (5&6) The defender then simultaneously forces the attacker's knife arm down behind his head, and sweeps his support leg to bring him down.

5

6

Wing Chun Against an Overhead Strike

(1-3) The defender stands with his hands alongside his body. The attacker steps in with an overhead strike with a club. The defender steps slightly to the left, using a right bil sao to deflect the stick. (4) He then brings his right arm over the stick. (5) Then the defender brings his left arm under the stick and over the attacker's right wrist. (6) The defender holds the attacker's right wrist and at the same time pushes sharply with the left hand to the attacker's right elbow. (7) The defender takes away the attacker's stick and (8) finishes off with a strike to the attacker's knee with the stick.

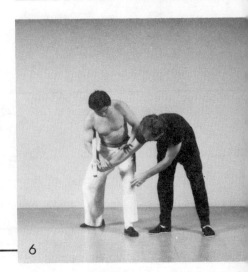

1

Jeet Kune Do Against an Overhead Strike

(1&2) The attacker attempts a downward swing. (3&4) The defender evades the attack

2

by stepping back, and then (5) counters with a side kick to the midsection.

Wing Chun Against a Backhand Swing

(1-2) The defender stands with his arms alongside his body. The attacker steps in with a backhand swing, and the defender uses a double pak sao to block it. As his right hand makes contact with the attacker's right hand, his left hand makes contact with the attacker's right wrist. (3) The defender steps to his left and slips his left hand behind the attacker's right elbow, giving it a hard push to bring the attacker to the ground.

Jeet Kune Do Against a Backhand Swing

(1&2) As the attacker prepares for a backhand swing with the club, the defender immediately steps in to immobilize the arm, and (3) executes a punch to the midsection.

Wing Chun Against an Overhead Attack From Behind

(1) The defender stands with his arms alongside his body, and the attacker places his left hand on the defender's right shoulder, with the stick in his right hand. (2) The attacker uses an overhead strike. The defender turns to the right, using a double pak sao to stop the strike as the left hand makes contact with the stick close to the attacker's right wrist. (3) The defender then slips his left hand to the left of the stick, (4) grabs the stick, and gives it a good yank to dislodge and capture it. (5) The defender then side kicks to the attacker's ribs.

Jeet Kune Do Against a Rear Club Attack

(1) The attacker approaches from behind the defender and grabs his shoulder for a club attack. (2&3) The defender turns, and executes a backfist strike to the attacker's face.

182

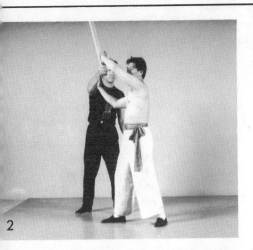

2

4

5

2

3

Wing Chun Against
a Diagonal Forearm Attack

(1) The defender stands with his arms at his sides. (2&3) The attacker moves in with a right diagonal forearm attack, and the defender uses both hands to stop the staff at the middle. (4) The defender turns the staff anti-clockwise, and at the same time side kicks to the attacker's knee. (5) The defender then strikes the attacker's neck with the staff.

Jeet Kune Do Against a Swing Attack

(1) The attacker attempts a swinging attack with the staff. The defender evades the staff with a quick retreat, and (2) allows the staff to pass in front of him to the other side. He then (3) steps in and delivers a low side kick to the attacker's knee.

5

3

Wing Chun Against a Forward Thrust Attack

(1) The defender stands with his arms at his sides. (2&3) The attacker steps in with a forward thrust attack. The defender sidesteps by stepping across with his left foot to the right, and at the same time, pushes the staff away from

his body. (4) The defender grabs hold of the staff with his left hand, and at the same time, palm strikes to the attacker's temple. (5) He then follows up with a side palm strike to the attacker's jaw.

Jeet Kune Do Against a Forward Thrust Attack

(1) The defender faces the attacker from the on-guard position. (2) The attacker attempts a forward thrust attack with the staff. The defender

sidesteps to the outside and grabs the staff. (3) He uses the staff for leverage as he executes a leg sweep, and (4) brings down the attacker.

Wing Chun Against
an Overhead Strike

(1) The defender stands with his arms at his sides. (2&3) The attacker steps in with an overhead strike, and the defender uses a bil sao to block the staff at the middle. (4&5) The defender then pushes the staff down with his left hand, hooks his right hand behind the attacker's neck, and moves up with a right knee to his face.

3

Jeet Kune Do Against
an Overhead Swing

(1&2) The attacker attempts an overhead swing with the staff. (3) The defender steps forward to intercept and trap the attacker's upper arm, then follows through with an uppercut punch to the midsection.

5

3